SRA
OPEN COURT
READING

Just Jam

A Division of The **McGraw·Hill** Companies

Columbus, Ohio

www.sra4kids.com

SRA/McGraw-Hill

A Division of The **McGraw·Hill** *Companies*

Printed in the United States of America.

Send all inquiries to:
SRA/McGraw-Hill
8787 Orion Place
Columbus, OH 43240-4027

ISBN 0-07-569446-8
3 4 5 6 7 8 9 DBH 05 04 03 02

"Did Jill pack a snack?" said Jim.

"Yes, ham on a bun," said Jan.

"Did Jack pack a snack?" said Jim.

"Yes, jam in a jug," said Jan.

"Jam in a jug? Just jam in a jug?" said Jim.

"Yes, Jack is a jam man," said Jan.